SAFE ON THE
PLAYGROUND

PowerKiDS press

New York

VICTOR BLAINE

Published in 2017 by The Rosen Publishing Group, Inc.
29 East 21st Street, New York, NY 10010

First Edition

Editor: Theresa Morlock
Book Design: Reann Nye

Photo Credits: Cover (background), p. 24 (playground) senee sriyota/Shutterstock.com; cover, p. 1 (girl) wavebreakmedia/Shutterstock.com; p. 5 Pressmaster/Shutterstock.com; p. 6 Portra Images/DigitalVision/ Getty Images; pp. 9, 24 (grownup) Erik Isakson/Blend Images/Getty Images; p. 10 TinnaPong/Shutterstock.com; pp. 13, 24 (swings) karelnoppe/Shutterstock.com; p. 14 Pamela Moore/E+/Getty Images; p. 17 TaPhotograph/ Moment Open/Getty Images; p. 18 Beau Lark/Corbis/VCG/Corbis/Getty Images; p. 21 Syda Productions/ Getty Images; p. 22 Christopher Futcher/E+/Getty Images.

Cataloging-in-Publication Data

Names: Blaine, Victor.
Title: Safe on the playground / Victor Blaine.
Description: New York : PowerKids Press, 2017. | Series: Safety smarts | Includes index.
Identifiers: ISBN 9781499427851 (pbk.) | ISBN 9781499429947 (library bound) | ISBN 9781499428674 (6 pack)
Subjects: LCSH: Playgrounds–Safety measures–Juvenile literature.
Classification: LCC GV424.B53 2017 | DDC 796.068–dc23

Manufactured in the United States of America

CPSIA Compliance Information: Batch #BW17PK: For Further Information contact Rosen Publishing, New York, New York at 1-800-237-9932

CONTENTS

We love the **playground**!

5

How can we be safe?

We go with **grownups**.

9

We don't climb too high.

We sit on the **swings**.

13

We wait our turn.

We bring water to drink.

17

We don't throw rocks.

We are nice to others.

21

22

We have fun!

WORDS TO KNOW

grownup

playground

swings

INDEX

WEBSITES

Due to the changing nature of Internet links, PowerKids Press has developed an online list of websites related to the subject of this book. This site is updated regularly. Please use this link to access the list: www.powerkidslinks.com/safe/play

24